Dedication

I want to dedicate this book to anyone who is struggling with self doubt, and uncertainty.

If anyone hasn't told you today, I will....

YOU ARE LOVED, AND YOU ARE ENOUGH.

THE SERENE PATH: Mastering The Art Of Guided Meditation

By: Tamara Wood

Title: The Serene Path: Mastering the Art of Guided Meditation

Table of Contents:

Note: The book will consist of detailed instructions, practical tips, personal anecdotes, and scientific research to provide a comprehensive guide to the art of guided meditation. It will cater to beginners and experienced practitioners alike, offering a wealth of information and techniques to deepen their meditation practice and experience the profound benefits of guided meditation in various aspects of life.

Chapter 1: Understanding Guided Meditation

1.1 What is Guided Meditation?

Guided meditation is a practice that involves following the verbal guidance of a facilitator or listening to recorded instructions to enter a state of deep relaxation, focus, and self-awareness. It is a form of meditation that utilizes the power of storytelling, visualization, and soothing guidance to lead practitioners through a journey of the mind and senses. Guided meditation provides a structured pathway for individuals to explore their inner world, access their subconscious mind, and experience a state of calm and tranquility.

1.2 The Benefits of Guided Meditation

Guided meditation offers a wide range of benefits for individuals seeking to improve their mental, emotional, and physical well-being. Some of the key benefits include:

1.2.1 Relaxation and Stress Reduction: Guided meditation helps release tension, reduce anxiety, and induce a state of deep relaxation. By following the guided instructions, practitioners can let go of worries and immerse themselves in a calming inner experience.

1.2.2 Increased Self-Awareness: Through guided meditation, individuals can cultivate a deeper understanding of their thoughts, emotions, and patterns of behavior. This self-awareness allows for personal growth, self-reflection, and making conscious choices aligned with one's values.

1.2.3 Improved Focus and Concentration: Guided meditation enhances mental clarity and improves the ability to concentrate. Regular practice strengthens the attention muscle, enabling practitioners to stay present and focused in various aspects of life.

1.2.4 Emotional Healing and Well-being: Guided meditation provides a safe space to explore and heal emotional wounds, traumas, and negative emotions.

It promotes self-compassion, forgiveness, and a sense of inner peace, fostering emotional well-being.

1.2.5 Enhanced Creativity and Intuition: By accessing the deeper layers of the mind, guided meditation stimulates creativity and intuition. It helps individuals tap into their innate wisdom and unlock new perspectives, ideas, and solutions.

1.2.6 Physical Health Benefits: Guided meditation has been linked to various physical health benefits, including reduced blood pressure, improved sleep quality, boosted immune function, and alleviation of chronic pain. It promotes a mind-body connection that supports overall well-being.

1.3 How Guided Meditation Differs from Traditional Meditation

While traditional meditation typically involves focusing on the breath or an object to quiet the mind, guided meditation takes a different approach. Here are some ways in which guided meditation differs:

1.3.1 External Guidance: In guided meditation, practitioners follow the instructions and guidance provided by a facilitator or a recorded voice. This external guidance leads them through visualizations, storytelling, and prompts, making the practice more structured and accessible.

1.3.2 Imagery and Visualization: Guided meditation often incorporates vivid imagery and visualization techniques to engage the senses and create a rich inner experience. These visualizations help deepen relaxation, stimulate the imagination, and evoke positive emotions.

1.3.3 Storytelling and Narratives: Guided meditation frequently employs storytelling elements to captivate the mind and transport practitioners to different mental landscapes. Narratives can be metaphorical, symbolic, or inspired by real-life experiences, offering a unique journey within the meditation practice.

1.3.4 Varied Themes and Intentions: Guided meditation allows for a wide range of themes and intentions, such as self-discovery, healing, stress relief, or manifestation. This versatility caters to different needs and preferences, making the practice more adaptable and engaging.

1.4 Setting Intentions for Your Practice

Before beginning a guided meditation practice, it is essential to set clear intentions. Intentions act as a compass, guiding your focus and shaping the desired outcomes of your meditation journey. Here are some tips for setting intentions:

1.4.1 Reflect on Your Needs: Take a moment to identify the areas of your life where you seek growth, healing, or transformation. Reflect on your emotional well-being, relationships, personal goals, or spiritual development. Choose an intention that resonates with your current needs.

1.4.2 Keep it Positive and Present: Frame your intention in positive language and focus on the present moment. For example, instead of saying, "I want to overcome my anxiety," rephrase it as, "I am cultivating inner calm and peace." This helps create a sense of empowerment and reinforces the belief that your intention is attainable.

1.4.3 Make it Personal and Meaningful: Your intention should be personal and meaningful to you. It should align with your values, aspirations, and inner growth. By connecting with your intention at a deeper level, you strengthen your commitment to the practice and increase its effectiveness.

1.4.4 Write it Down: Consider writing your intention on a piece of paper or in a journal. This physical representation of your intention can serve as a reminder and anchor during your guided meditation sessions.

1.4.5 Revisit and Revise: As you progress on your meditation journey, periodically revisit and revise your intentions. As you achieve certain goals or experience shifts in your life, adjust your intentions accordingly to stay aligned with your evolving needs.

Setting intentions for your guided meditation practice adds depth and purpose to your sessions. It helps you direct your energy, attention, and focus toward the desired outcomes, enhancing the transformative potential of the practice.

In the next chapter, we will explore the process of creating a sacred space, a nurturing environment that supports your guided meditation practice.

Chapter 2: Creating a Sacred Space

2.1 Finding the Perfect Location

When embarking on your guided meditation journey, it is essential to find a suitable location that promotes a sense of peace and tranquility. Here are some considerations when finding the perfect location for your sacred space:

2.1.1 Quiet and Distraction-Free: Choose a space where you can minimize external distractions and interruptions. Find a room or area in your home where you can shut the door or communicate with others to maintain a quiet environment during your practice.

2.1.2 Comfortable and Relaxing: Select a location that allows you to sit or lie down comfortably for the duration of your guided meditation. Consider using a cushion, yoga mat, or meditation chair to support your posture and provide physical comfort.

2.1.3 Natural Light or Dim Lighting: If possible, choose a space with access to natural light. Natural light can create a soothing ambiance and enhance your connection to the outside world. Alternatively, you can opt for dim lighting or use candles or soft lamps to create a serene atmosphere.

2.2 Creating an Atmosphere of Tranquility

Once you have found the ideal location for your sacred space, it's time to cultivate an atmosphere of tranquility that supports your guided meditation practice. Here are some ways to create a peaceful environment:

2.2.1 Clean and Clutter-Free: Clear the space of any clutter or unnecessary items. A clean and organized environment promotes mental clarity and allows for better focus during your meditation practice.

2.2.2 Pleasant Scents: Consider using essential oils, incense, or candles with calming scents such as lavender, sandalwood, or frankincense. Pleasant aromas can help relax the mind and create a sensory anchor for your meditation practice.

2.2.3 Soft Colors and Textures: Choose soothing colors for your sacred space, such as pastels or earth tones. Soft textures, such as pillows, blankets, or a cozy rug, can add a sense of comfort and warmth to your space.

2.2.4 Soundscapes or Ambient Music: Ambient music or nature sounds, like flowing water or gentle rain, can create a peaceful auditory backdrop for your meditation practice. Experiment with different sounds to find what resonates with you.

2.3 Incorporating Elements of Nature

Bringing elements of nature into your sacred space can deepen your connection to the natural world and enhance your meditation experience. Consider the following:

2.3.1 Indoor Plants: Introduce houseplants or fresh flowers to your sacred space. Plants not only add beauty but also help purify the air and create a sense of vitality and grounding.

2.3.2 Natural Materials: Incorporate natural materials, such as wood, stone, or seashells, into your space. These materials can evoke a sense of earthiness and connect you with the grounding energy of nature.

2.3.3 Nature-inspired Art or Imagery: Hang or display artwork, photographs, or images that depict landscapes, animals, or natural scenes. These visual cues can transport your mind to serene natural settings during your guided meditations.

2.4 Enhancing Your Space with Meaningful Objects

Adding meaningful objects to your sacred space can infuse it with personal significance and create a deeper sense of connection. Here are some ideas:

2.4.1 Altar or Shrine: Create a small altar or shrine with objects that hold spiritual or personal significance to you. It could include photographs, crystals, statues, or items representing your beliefs, values, or aspirations.

2.4.2 Inspirational Quotes or Affirmations: Display inspiring quotes, affirmations, or mantras that resonate with you. These reminders can serve as focal points for reflection and motivation during your guided meditation practice.

2.4.3 Personal Mementos: Include items that hold sentimental value, such as a cherished piece of jewelry, a meaningful keepsake, or a symbol of a significant life event. These objects can evoke positive emotions and deep connections.

2.4.4 Ritual Objects: If you engage in specific rituals or ceremonies, incorporate the relevant objects into your sacred space. This could include candles, feathers, bells, or any other items that symbolize your spiritual or cultural practices.

Remember, the purpose of creating a sacred space is to establish an environment that supports your guided meditation practice and helps you cultivate a deeper connection with yourself. Customize your space according to your preferences and let it reflect your unique journey.

In the next chapter, we will explore the necessary steps for preparing yourself before engaging in guided meditation, including cultivating a mindful mindset and choosing the right time to meditate.

Chapter 3: Preparing for Guided Meditation

3.1 Cultivating a Mindful Mindset

Before beginning your guided meditation practice, it is essential to cultivate a mindful mindset. This mindset helps create a receptive and present state of mind. Here are some practices to cultivate a mindful mindset:

3.1.1 Settle the Mind: Take a few moments to settle your mind by finding a comfortable position and closing your eyes. Bring your attention to the present moment and let go of any thoughts or distractions. Allow yourself to be fully present and open to the experience.

3.1.2 Let Go of Expectations: Release any expectations or judgments about your meditation practice. Approach it with a sense of curiosity and openness, without attaching yourself to any specific outcomes. Allow yourself to embrace whatever arises during the meditation without resistance.

3.1.3 Non-Judgmental Awareness: Practice observing your thoughts, emotions, and bodily sensations without judgment. Be an impartial witness to whatever arises within you. Embrace all experiences with compassion and acceptance, knowing that they are part of the meditation journey.

3.1.4 Cultivate Gratitude: Take a moment to express gratitude for this opportunity to engage in guided meditation. Appreciate the time and space you have created for self-care and inner exploration. Cultivating gratitude sets a positive tone for your practice.

3.2 Choosing the Right Time to Meditate

Selecting the right time for your guided meditation practice can significantly impact its effectiveness. Consider the following when choosing the optimal time:

3.2.1 Consistency: Establish a regular meditation schedule by choosing a consistent time each day. Consistency helps build a habit and allows your mind and body to become attuned to the practice.

3.2.2 Personal Preference: Choose a time that aligns with your natural rhythms and personal preferences. Some people find morning meditation energizing and grounding, while others prefer the evening to unwind and relax. Experiment with different times to find what works best for you.

3.2.3 Quiet and Calm: Select a time when your surroundings are relatively quiet and free from distractions. This could be early in the morning before others wake up or in the evening when the day's activities have settled down.

3.2.4 Avoid Heavy Meals: It is advisable to avoid practicing guided meditation immediately after consuming a heavy meal. Digestion can divert energy and attention, making it more challenging to focus during meditation. Opt for a light snack if needed before your practice.

3.3 Clothing and Posture

Creating physical comfort during guided meditation contributes to a more focused and relaxed state. Consider the following clothing and posture tips:

3.3.1 Comfortable Clothing: Wear loose, comfortable clothing that allows for unrestricted movement and breath. Avoid tight-fitting attire that may cause discomfort or restrict your circulation.

3.3.2 Sitting Posture: If you choose to sit during your guided meditation, find a position that supports an upright yet relaxed posture. This could include sitting on a cushion, using a meditation bench, or sitting cross-legged on a mat. Align your spine, relax your shoulders, and find a position that feels balanced and stable.

3.3.3 Lying Down Posture: If you prefer to lie down during your guided meditation, find a comfortable surface such as a yoga mat or a comfortable bed. Ensure that your body is supported and relaxed, with your spine in a neutral position.

3.3.4 Experiment and Adjust: Explore different sitting or lying down positions to find what works best for you. Everyone's body is unique, so adjust your posture as needed to maintain physical comfort and avoid unnecessary strain.

3.4 Breathwork and Relaxation Techniques

Preparing your body and mind for guided meditation can be enhanced by incorporating breathwork and relaxation techniques. Consider the following:

3.4.1 Deep Breathing: Take a few moments to focus on your breath. Inhale deeply through your nose, allowing your abdomen to expand, and exhale fully through your mouth, releasing any tension or stress. Deep breathing calms the nervous system and prepares the mind for relaxation.

3.4.2 Progressive Muscle Relaxation: Perform a body scan and progressively relax each muscle group from head to toe or vice versa. Tense and release each muscle group, allowing any accumulated tension to dissolve, and promoting a sense of deep relaxation.

3.4.3 Grounding Techniques: Engage in grounding techniques such as visualizing roots extending from your body into the earth or connecting with the stability and support of the ground beneath you. Grounding techniques help establish a sense of stability and presence.

3.4.4 Body Awareness: Bring attention to your body and scan for any areas of tension or discomfort. Take a moment to release and let go of any physical sensations that arise. Cultivating body awareness promotes relaxation and helps establish a connection between mind and body.

By incorporating these practices into your pre-meditation routine, you set the stage for a more focused, relaxed, and enriching guided meditation experience.

In the next chapter, we will delve into the different types of guided meditation techniques and explore how to choose the right one for your needs and preferences.

Chapter 4: The Art of Guided Meditation

4.1 Selecting a Guided Meditation Technique

Guided meditation encompasses various techniques that cater to different purposes and preferences. Consider the following when selecting a guided meditation technique:

4.1.1 Mindfulness Meditation: This technique involves focusing your attention on the present moment, observing your thoughts, emotions, and bodily sensations without judgment. Mindfulness meditation cultivates awareness and helps develop a non-reactive and accepting mindset.

4.1.2 Loving-Kindness Meditation: Also known as Metta meditation, this technique involves cultivating feelings of love, compassion, and goodwill toward oneself and others. It involves reciting or silently repeating phrases of well-wishing and sending positive intentions to yourself, loved ones, and all beings.

4.1.3 Body Scan Meditation: This technique involves systematically scanning your body from head to toe, bringing awareness to each body part and observing any sensations or tension. Body scan meditation promotes relaxation, body awareness, and a sense of deep connection with oneself.

4.1.4 Visualization Meditation: Visualization techniques involve creating vivid mental images and using the power of imagination to enhance your meditation experience. Visualization can be used for healing, goal manifestation, or creating a serene mental landscape.

4.1.5 Guided Imagery: Guided imagery involves following a narrative or script that takes you on a journey through various landscapes, scenarios, or situations. It taps into your imagination to promote relaxation, insight, and personal growth.

4.2 Developing a Connection with Your Inner Guide

In guided meditation, your inner guide is your intuitive and wise self that helps navigate your inner world. Cultivating a connection with your inner guide enhances the depth and effectiveness of your practice. Here's how to develop a connection with your inner guide:

4.2.1 Set the Intention: Before each guided meditation session, set the intention to connect with your inner guide and receive guidance and insights.

4.2.2 Trust Your Intuition: During meditation, listen to your intuition and trust the messages and guidance that arise. Avoid doubting or dismissing your inner wisdom.

4.2.3 Create Dialogue: Engage in a dialogue with your inner guide. Ask questions, seek guidance, and listen attentively for responses or insights.

4.2.4 Journaling: After your guided meditation, take a few moments to journal your experiences, messages, and insights received from your inner guide. Journaling helps deepen your connection and allows for reflection and integration.

4.3 Choosing the Right Guided Meditation Script

The selection of a guided meditation script is crucial for an enriching meditation experience. Consider the following when choosing a guided meditation script:

4.3.1 Alignment with Intentions: Choose a script that aligns with your specific intentions and goals. Whether it's relaxation, healing, self-discovery, or personal growth, ensure that the script resonates with your needs.

4.3.2 Authenticity of the Guide: Select guided meditations led by experienced and reputable meditation guides or instructors. Research their credentials, reviews, and expertise to ensure the quality and effectiveness of the script.

4.3.3 Voice and Tone: Pay attention to the voice and tone of the guide. Choose a voice that is soothing, calming, and resonates with you. The guide's tone should help you relax and feel at ease.

4.3.4 Length and Format: Consider the length of the guided meditation script and whether it fits your available time and attention span. Some scripts may be shorter for quick relaxation, while others may be longer for a more immersive experience.

4.4 Enhancing Visualization and Imagination

Visualization and imagination are powerful tools in guided meditation. Here's how you can enhance these aspects of your practice:

4.4.1 Engage the Senses: Incorporate sensory details in your visualization, such as the sights, sounds, smells, and textures of the imagined scenario. Engaging the senses makes the visualization more vivid and immersive.

4.4.2 Emotional Connection: Connect with the emotions associated with your visualization. Visualize how you would feel in the imagined scenario, whether it's a sense of peace, joy, or fulfillment. Emotions add depth and resonance to your experience.

4.4.3 Use Symbolism: Incorporate symbolic objects or imagery that hold personal meaning for you. Symbols can represent qualities, aspirations, or intentions, and they deepen the impact of the visualization.

4.4.4 Practice Regularly: Regular practice strengthens your visualization and imagination abilities. Over time, you will become more adept at creating detailed and vibrant mental images during guided meditation.

4.5 Incorporating Affirmations and Mantras

Affirmations and mantras are powerful tools for cultivating positive thoughts and shifting your mindset. Consider the following when incorporating affirmations and mantras into your guided meditation:

4.5.1 Choose Positive Statements: Select affirmations or mantras that reflect the qualities or states of being you wish to embody. Ensure that they are positively framed and resonate with your intentions.

4.5.2 Repetition and Internalization: Repeat the affirmations or mantras silently or aloud during your guided meditation. Allow the words to sink into your consciousness, internalizing their positive influence.

4.5.3 Align with the Present Moment: Phrase your affirmations or mantras in the present tense to align them with the power of the present moment. This helps reinforce the belief that the desired qualities or states of being are already within you.

4.5.4 Emotional Connection: Feel the emotions associated with the affirmations or mantras as you repeat them. Connect with the positive feelings they evoke, allowing them to permeate your being.

4.6 Harnessing the Power of Music and Sound

Music and sound can significantly enhance your guided meditation experience. Consider the following when harnessing the power of music and sound:

4.6.1 Select Calming and Soothing Music: Choose instrumental music or ambient soundscapes that promote relaxation and create a tranquil atmosphere. Avoid music with distracting lyrics or harsh tones that may disrupt your focus.

4.6.2 Nature Sounds: Incorporate nature sounds such as gentle rain, flowing water, or bird songs into your guided meditation. These sounds evoke a sense of peace, connectedness, and harmony with the natural world.

4.6.3 Binaural Beats and Brainwave Entrainment: Explore the use of binaural beats or brainwave entrainment audios that synchronize with specific brainwave frequencies associated with deep relaxation or heightened focus. These audios can help induce desired mental states during meditation.

4.6.4 Sound Healing Instruments: Consider incorporating sound healing instruments such as singing bowls, chimes, or gongs into your guided meditation. The resonant vibrations of these instruments can promote relaxation, balance, and energetic alignment.

Experiment with different combinations of music and sound to find what resonates with you and enhances your guided meditation experience.

In the next chapter, we will explore techniques for deepening your guided meditation practice, including methods for quieting the mind, cultivating mindfulness, and working with challenges that may arise during meditation.

Chapter 5: Exploring Different Meditation Themes

Meditation offers a wide range of themes and focuses that cater to various aspects of personal growth and well-being. In this chapter, we will explore different meditation themes and their benefits:

5.1 Self-Discovery and Personal Growth

Meditation can be a powerful tool for self-discovery and personal growth. By turning inward and exploring your thoughts, emotions, and beliefs, you can gain deeper insights into yourself and uncover hidden potentials. Guided meditations focused on self-discovery may include journaling prompts, visualization exercises, and introspective questions.

Benefits:

- Increased self-awareness
- Enhanced clarity and insight
- Improved decision-making

- Uncovering and embracing personal strengths and weaknesses
- Cultivating a sense of purpose and authenticity

5.2 Healing and Rejuvenation

Guided meditations focused on healing and rejuvenation can support physical, emotional, and mental well-being. These meditations often incorporate visualization, breathwork, and relaxation techniques to promote relaxation, release stress, and facilitate the body's natural healing processes.

Benefits:

- Stress reduction and relaxation
- Improved sleep quality
- Enhanced immune function
- Accelerated healing and recovery
- Emotional healing and release

5.3 Stress Relief and Relaxation

In our fast-paced world, stress relief and relaxation are essential for overall well-being. Guided meditations focused on stress relief and relaxation aim to calm the mind, release tension, and cultivate a state of inner peace. These meditations often incorporate deep breathing, body scan techniques, and soothing visualizations.

Benefits:

- Reduced stress and anxiety
- Increased relaxation and calmness
- Improved focus and concentration
- Lowered blood pressure and heart rate
- Enhanced overall well-being

5.4 Cultivating Compassion and Gratitude

Meditations centered around compassion and gratitude promote a positive mindset and foster connection with oneself and others. These meditations often involve loving-kindness practices, where you send well-wishes and compassion to yourself, loved ones, and all beings. Gratitude meditations focus on cultivating a sense of appreciation for the present moment and the blessings in life.

Benefits:

- Cultivation of empathy and compassion
- Increased feelings of interconnectedness
- Reduction of negative emotions and judgment
- Greater resilience and emotional well-being
- Heightened sense of gratitude and contentment

5.5 Manifestation and Abundance

Guided meditations focused on manifestation and abundance help align your thoughts, emotions, and intentions with your desired goals and aspirations. These meditations often involve visualization, affirmation, and energetic alignment techniques to harness the power of the mind and attract positive experiences and abundance into your life.

Benefits:

- Clarification of goals and desires
- Heightened focus and intention-setting
- Increased confidence and self-belief
- Amplified manifestation abilities
- Cultivation of abundance mindset

5.6 Connecting with Spirituality and Higher Consciousness

For those seeking a deeper spiritual connection and exploration of higher consciousness, guided meditations can serve as a gateway to transcendental experiences. These meditations may involve connecting with spiritual guides, exploring the realms of consciousness, or contemplating philosophical concepts.

Benefits:

- Deepened spiritual connection
- Expanded awareness and consciousness
- Transcendence of limiting beliefs and perspectives

- Enhanced intuition and spiritual guidance
- Greater sense of purpose and interconnectedness

Explore different meditation themes and choose those that resonate with your current needs and aspirations. Remember that these themes are not mutually exclusive, and you can explore multiple themes depending on your evolving journey.

In the next chapter, we will delve into techniques for overcoming challenges and maintaining a consistent guided meditation practice.

Chapter 6: Guided Meditation Techniques for Daily Life

Incorporating guided meditation into your daily life can bring a sense of calm, clarity, and balance to your routines and activities. In this chapter, we will explore various guided meditation techniques specifically tailored for different aspects of daily life:

6.1 Morning Meditations to Start Your Day

Starting your day with a guided meditation sets a positive tone and promotes a sense of presence and intention. Consider the following morning meditation techniques:

6.1.1 Gratitude Meditation: Express gratitude for the new day and set a positive tone for the day ahead. Reflect on things you are grateful for, both big and small, and cultivate a sense of appreciation and joy.

6.1.2 Intentions and Affirmations: Set your intentions for the day and recite affirmations that align with your goals and aspirations. Visualize yourself moving through the day with purpose and clarity.

6.1.3 Energizing Visualization: Engage in a visualization that invigorates and energizes you for the day. Imagine vibrant energy flowing through your body, revitalizing your mind, and preparing you for a productive and fulfilling day.

6.2 Meditations for Stressful Situations

In times of stress or challenging situations, guided meditations can help you find calm and navigate through difficulties. Try the following techniques:

6.2.1 Breathing Exercises: Focus on your breath and practice deep, conscious breathing. Use techniques like square breathing or 4-7-8 breathing to regulate your breath and induce relaxation.

6.2.2 Body Scan and Relaxation: Perform a quick body scan to identify areas of tension or stress. Bring your awareness to those areas and consciously release any tension, allowing your body to relax and unwind.

6.2.3 Grounding Meditation: Connect with the present moment by grounding yourself. Visualize roots extending from your body into the earth, anchoring you and providing stability and support.

6.3 Meditative Tools for Enhanced Productivity

Guided meditations can also be used as tools for increased focus, creativity, and productivity. Consider incorporating the following techniques into your work or study routines:

6.3.1 Mindful Breathing Breaks: Take short breaks throughout your work or study sessions to focus on your breath and bring your attention back to the present moment. This helps prevent overwhelm and promotes clarity.

6.3.2 Visualization for Goal Achievement: Visualize yourself successfully accomplishing your tasks and achieving your goals. See yourself working efficiently and effortlessly, feeling motivated and inspired.

6.3.3 Flow State Meditation: Tap into the flow state by engaging in a guided meditation that encourages a sense of deep focus and immersion in your work. Cultivate a state of mindfulness and let go of distractions.

6.4 Meditations for Restful Sleep

Guided meditations can help prepare your mind and body for a restful night's sleep. Incorporate the following techniques into your bedtime routine:

6.4.1 Relaxation and Breathwork: Engage in relaxation techniques such as deep breathing and progressive muscle relaxation to release tension and promote a state of calm before sleep.

6.4.2 Guided Body Scan: Scan your body from head to toe, bringing awareness to each body part and consciously releasing any lingering tension. This promotes physical relaxation and prepares you for sleep.

6.4.3 Gratitude and Letting Go: Reflect on the events of the day and let go of any negative or stressful experiences. Cultivate gratitude for the positive moments and focus on feelings of peace and contentment.

6.5 Integrating Mindfulness into Everyday Activities

Guided meditations can be incorporated into your daily activities to cultivate mindfulness and presence. Consider the following techniques:

6.5.1 Mindful Eating: Engage in a guided meditation while eating, bringing awareness to the flavors, textures, and sensations of each bite. Slow down and savor the experience fully.

6.5.2 Walking Meditation: Practice guided meditation while walking, focusing on each step, the sensations in your body, and the surrounding environment. Cultivate a sense of presence and appreciation for the act of walking.

6.5.3 Mindful Pause: Take brief moments throughout the day to pause, close your eyes if possible, and engage in a short, guided meditation to bring your attention back to the present moment and release any tension or stress.

By incorporating these guided meditation techniques into your daily life, you can experience increased focus, relaxation, and overall well-being. Experiment with different techniques and adapt them to suit your preferences and schedule.

In the next chapter, we will explore the role of self-reflection and journaling in deepening your guided meditation practice and fostering personal growth.

Chapter 7: Overcoming Challenges in Guided Meditation

Guided meditation, like any practice, can come with its own set of challenges. In this chapter, we will explore common challenges that may arise during guided meditation and techniques to overcome them:

7.1 Dealing with Restlessness and Distractions

Restlessness and distractions are common challenges in meditation. Here are some strategies to address them:

7.1.1 Gentle Refocusing: When you notice your mind wandering or becoming restless, gently bring your attention back to the present moment and the guidance provided in the meditation. Refocus without judgment or frustration.

7.1.2 Anchoring Techniques: Use anchor points, such as your breath or a specific sensation in your body, to ground yourself and bring your attention back whenever distractions arise. This helps maintain focus and stability.

7.1.3 Labeling and Letting Go: Label any distracting thoughts or emotions as "thinking" or "feeling" without getting caught up in their content. Allow them to pass by like clouds in the sky and return your attention to the meditation.

7.1.4 Environmental Adjustments: Minimize external distractions by finding a quiet space, using earplugs or headphones, or creating a peaceful atmosphere that supports your practice.

7.2 Navigating Resistance and Emotional Blocks

Resistance and emotional blocks can arise during guided meditation. Here's how to navigate them:

7.2.1 Gentle Exploration: Approach resistance or emotional blocks with curiosity and compassion. Allow yourself to gently explore the underlying emotions or thoughts that may be present without judgment.

7.2.2 Loving-Kindness Meditation: Engage in loving-kindness practices to cultivate compassion and send well-wishes to yourself and any emotional challenges you may be experiencing. This can help soften resistance and foster emotional healing.

7.2.3 Emotional Release: If emotions arise during meditation, allow them to surface without suppressing or clinging to them. Allow yourself to feel and experience the emotions fully, offering yourself kindness and acceptance.

7.2.4 Seek Support: If you find yourself consistently struggling with emotional blocks or resistance, consider seeking support from a meditation teacher, therapist, or trusted mentor who can provide guidance and assistance.

7.3 Letting Go of Expectations and Judgments

Letting go of expectations and judgments is crucial for a fruitful guided meditation practice. Consider the following techniques:

7.3.1 Non-Striving Attitude: Approach meditation with a non-striving attitude, letting go of the need to achieve specific outcomes or experiences. Instead, cultivate a sense of openness and curiosity toward the present moment.

7.3.2 Self-Compassion: Practice self-compassion by acknowledging that meditation is a journey, and that each session is an opportunity for growth and self-discovery. Let go of self-judgment and embrace self-acceptance.

7.3.3 Reframing Thoughts: Notice any expectations or judgments that arise and gently reframe them. Instead of labeling thoughts as "good" or "bad," view them as passing phenomena and refocus your attention on the meditation.

7.3.4 Gratitude for Effort: Cultivate gratitude for your commitment to guided meditation and the effort you put into your practice. Acknowledge that every moment spent in meditation contributes to your personal growth and well-being.

7.4 Cultivating Patience and Persistence

Patience and persistence are essential qualities for a successful guided meditation practice. Consider these strategies:

7.4.1 Gentle Discipline: Approach meditation with a sense of gentle discipline, understanding that consistency and regularity are key to progress. Set aside dedicated time for meditation and honor that commitment.

7.4.2 Mindfulness of Progress: Cultivate mindfulness of the progress you make in your practice, even if it feels subtle. Notice the small shifts in your awareness, focus, or overall well-being, and let them fuel your motivation.

7.4.3 Celebrate Small Wins: Acknowledge and celebrate small victories along your meditation journey. Whether it's a longer period of focus or a deeper sense of calm, celebrate these milestones to stay motivated and encouraged.

7.4.4 Community Support: Connect with a community of fellow meditators who can provide support, encouragement, and accountability. Share your experiences, challenges, and successes with others who can relate to your journey.

Remember that overcoming challenges in guided meditation is part of the process. Embrace the journey with patience, persistence, and self-compassion. As you continue to cultivate your practice, you will develop valuable skills to navigate these challenges and experience the transformative power of guided meditation.

In the next chapter, we will explore the role of self-reflection and journaling in deepening your guided meditation practice and fostering personal growth.

Chapter 8: Taking Your Practice Further

Guided meditation is a dynamic practice that allows for continuous growth and exploration. In this chapter, we will delve into ways to take your guided meditation practice further and expand your skills:

8.1 Deepening Your Connection with Self

Deepening your connection with self is a transformative aspect of guided meditation. Here are some techniques to enhance this connection:

8.1.1 Inner Dialogue: Engage in inner dialogue during your guided meditation practice. Ask yourself introspective questions and listen for the responses that arise from within. This fosters self-awareness and deepens your understanding of yourself.

8.1.2 Body Sensations: Bring your attention to the sensations in your body during meditation. Notice any areas of tension, discomfort, or ease. Allow yourself to fully experience and explore these sensations, fostering a deeper connection with your physical being.

8.1.3 Journaling and Reflection: After each meditation session, take time to journal and reflect on your experiences. Write down any insights, thoughts, or emotions that surfaced during the practice. This self-reflection deepens your connection with self and encourages personal growth.

8.2 Exploring Advanced Visualization Techniques

Visualization is a powerful tool in guided meditation. Consider exploring advanced visualization techniques to expand your practice:

8.2.1 Multi-Sensory Visualization: Engage multiple senses in your visualizations. Imagine not only the sights but also the sounds, smells, textures, and tastes associated with the visualized scenario. This enhances the vividness and realism of your visualizations.

8.2.2 Time Travel Visualization: Explore the concept of time travel in your guided meditations. Visualize yourself in different time periods, exploring past memories or envisioning future possibilities. This technique offers insights, healing, and expanded perspectives.

8.2.3 Chakra Balancing: Incorporate chakra visualization into your practice. Visualize each chakra as a vibrant, spinning energy center within your body. Focus on balancing and harmonizing the energy flow in each chakra, fostering overall well-being and alignment.

8.3 Incorporating Breathwork and Body Awareness

Breathwork and body awareness techniques deepen your presence and connection with the physical body. Try the following approaches:

8.3.1 Conscious Breathwork: Explore various breathwork techniques such as alternate nostril breathing, breath retention, or deep belly breathing. These techniques bring awareness to the breath, regulate energy, and promote relaxation and focus.

8.3.2 Body Scan Meditation: Practice body scan meditations to cultivate a heightened sense of body awareness. Move your attention through different parts of your body, scanning for sensations, tension, or areas of relaxation. This practice promotes deep relaxation and presence.

8.3.3 Movement Meditation: Combine guided meditation with gentle movement, such as yoga or tai chi. Engage in mindful, slow movements, syncing your breath with each motion. This practice cultivates body awareness, mindfulness, and a sense of embodiment.

8.4 Expanding Your Meditation Repertoire

Expand your meditation repertoire by exploring new techniques and styles. This keeps your practice fresh and opens new avenues for growth:

8.4.1 Silent Meditation: Set aside time for silent meditation without external guidance. Allow yourself to sit in silence, focusing on your breath, sensations, or a chosen mantra. This practice deepens your ability to cultivate inner stillness and mindfulness.

8.4.2 Metta Meditation: Embrace metta, or loving-kindness meditation. Send well-wishes and compassion to yourself, loved ones, challenging individuals, and all beings. This practice cultivates a sense of empathy, connection, and universal love.

8.4.3 Sound Meditation: Explore sound-based meditation practices, such as chanting, singing bowls, or guided meditations with soundscapes. These practices harness the power of sound to promote relaxation, focus, and vibrational healing.

Continuously expand and evolve your guided meditation practice. Be open to exploring new techniques, deepening your connection with self, and incorporating advanced visualization, breathwork, and body awareness. Embrace the journey of self-discovery and personal growth that guided meditation offers.

In the final chapter, we will explore the integration of guided meditation into everyday life and how to sustain a consistent practice.

Chapter 9: Guided Meditation for Others

Guided meditation is not only a personal practice but also a powerful tool for sharing with others. In this chapter, we will explore various aspects of sharing guided meditation with loved ones, facilitating group meditation sessions, tailoring meditations for specific audiences, and the possibility of becoming a certified meditation instructor:

9.1 Sharing Guided Meditations with Loved Ones

Guided meditation can be a beautiful way to connect with and support your loved ones in their own meditation practice. Consider the following suggestions when sharing guided meditations with others:

9.1.1 Selecting Appropriate Meditations: Choose guided meditations that resonate with the interests and needs of your loved ones. Consider their preferences, goals, and areas of focus such as stress relief, self-compassion, or personal growth.

9.1.2 Creating Personalized Meditations: Customize guided meditations by incorporating personal anecdotes, specific affirmations, or visualizations that hold meaning for your loved ones. This personal touch enhances the relevance and impact of meditation.

9.1.3 Sharing Meditation Resources: Recommend meditation apps, websites, or books that offer a variety of guided meditations. Encourage your loved ones to explore different resources and find the ones that resonate with them.

9.1.4 Practicing Together: Set aside dedicated time to practice guided meditation together. Create a peaceful and comfortable environment and engage in a shared experience of meditation. This cultivates a sense of connection and supports each other's practice.

9.2 Facilitating Group Meditation Sessions

Facilitating group meditation sessions allows you to create a supportive and transformative environment for a collective meditation experience. Here's how to facilitate successful group meditation sessions:

9.2.1 Setting the Space: Prepare a serene and welcoming space for the group meditation. Arrange cushions, chairs, or mats in a way that promotes comfort and a sense of community. Consider incorporating elements such as candles, soft lighting, or calming scents.

9.2.2 Introducing the Session: Begin the group meditation by introducing the intention and theme of the session. Explain any specific instructions or guidelines for the practice, and create a safe and non-judgmental space for participants to engage in the meditation.

9.2.3 Guiding the Meditation: Lead the group through a guided meditation, providing clear and soothing instructions. Pay attention to the pace, tone of voice, and ensuring that participants feel supported throughout the practice.

9.2.4 Allowing Silence and Reflection: After the guided meditation, allow a few moments of silence for participants to reflect and integrate their experiences. Encourage sharing if individuals feel comfortable, fostering a sense of community and mutual support.

9.2.5 Closing the Session: Conclude the group meditation by offering words of gratitude, appreciation, and encouragement. Share any resources or suggestions for continuing the meditation practice in their daily lives.

9.3 Guided Meditations for Specific Audiences (Children, Seniors, etc.)

Guided meditation can be tailored to meet the specific needs and interests of different audiences. Consider the following guidelines when creating meditations for specific groups:

9.3.1 Children: Simplify the language and concepts in guided meditations for children. Incorporate playful visualizations, storytelling elements, or interactive exercises to engage their imagination and hold their attention.

9.3.2 Seniors: Adapt guided meditations for seniors by considering their physical comfort and any mobility limitations. Emphasize relaxation, mindfulness, and gratitude practices that promote overall well-being and inner peace.

9.3.3 Workplace: Develop guided meditations specifically designed for the workplace to support stress reduction, focus, and productivity. Include mindfulness exercises that can be practiced discreetly and easily integrated into work routines.

9.4 Becoming a Certified Meditation Instructor

If you have a deep passion for guided meditation and wish to share it with others on a professional level, becoming a certified meditation instructor may be a fulfilling path. Consider the following steps:

9.4.1 Research Certification Programs: Explore reputable meditation teacher training programs that align with your interests and values. Look for programs that provide comprehensive instruction on meditation techniques, teaching methodologies, and ethics.

9.4.2 Participate in Training: Enroll in a meditation teacher training program that resonates with you. Engage in the coursework, practical exercises, and supervised teaching opportunities to develop your skills and knowledge as a meditation instructor.

9.4.3 Gain Teaching Experience: After completing your training, gain teaching experience by offering guided meditation sessions to friends, family, or local communities. This hands-on experience helps you refine your teaching style and build confidence.

9.4.4 Continuing Education and Professional Development: Stay engaged in continuous education to deepen your understanding of meditation practices and stay updated with the latest research and developments in the field. Attend workshops, conferences, and advanced training programs to expand your expertise.

Becoming a certified meditation instructor allows you to share the transformative power of guided meditation with a broader audience and contribute to the well-being of others.

As you explore sharing guided meditation with loved ones, facilitating group sessions, tailoring meditations for specific audiences, or considering certification, remember that your genuine intention to support and uplift others is at the heart of this journey.

In the concluding chapter, we will reflect on the overall impact of guided meditation and provide guidance on sustaining a consistent practice.

Chapter 10: Living a Meditative Life

Guided meditation is not limited to the time spent in formal practice. It is a way of being—a transformative approach to life itself. In this final chapter, we will explore how to integrate the principles of guided meditation into your daily life and cultivate a meditative way of living:

10.1 Bringing Meditation into Daily Life

10.1.1 Mindful Awareness: Cultivate mindful awareness in your daily activities. Pay attention to the present moment, bringing a sense of curiosity and non-judgment to your experiences. Whether you're eating, walking, or engaging in routine tasks, bring a meditative quality to each moment.

10.1.2 Conscious Breathing: Use conscious breathing as an anchor to bring you back to the present moment throughout the day. Take a few intentional breaths whenever you feel stressed, overwhelmed, or disconnected. This simple practice helps you center yourself and find inner calm.

10.1.3 Mini Meditations: Incorporate short meditative breaks into your day. Take a few minutes to close your eyes, focus on your breath, and bring your attention inward. These mini meditations can be done anywhere, providing a moment of rejuvenation and clarity.

10.2 Applying Mindfulness to Relationships

10.2.1 Presence in Communication: Practice mindful listening and speaking in your interactions with others. Be fully present and attentive, giving your undivided attention to the person you are engaging with. This fosters deep connections, empathy, and understanding.

10.2.2 Compassionate Responses: Cultivate compassion and empathy in your relationships. Before reacting, take a moment to pause, reflect, and respond with kindness and understanding. This practice enhances the quality of your relationships and promotes harmony.

10.2.3 Letting Go of Judgment: Release judgment and embrace acceptance in your relationships. Recognize that everyone is on their own journey and has their own struggles. Practice non-judgmental awareness and foster an environment of acceptance and love.

10.3 Cultivating Gratitude and Compassion

10.3.1 Gratitude Practice: Cultivate a daily gratitude practice. Take time each day to reflect on the things you are grateful for. This practice shifts your focus to the positive aspects of life, cultivating joy and appreciation.

10.3.2 Loving-Kindness Meditation: Engage in loving-kindness meditation regularly. Send wishes of love, well-being, and happiness to yourself, loved ones, acquaintances, and even challenging individuals. This practice expands your capacity for compassion and fosters a sense of interconnectedness.

10.3.3 Acts of Kindness: Incorporate acts of kindness into your daily life. Small gestures, such as offering a helping hand or expressing genuine care, have a ripple effect of positivity and contribute to a more compassionate world.

10.4 Creating Rituals and Practices

10.4.1 Morning and Evening Rituals: Establish mindful rituals to begin and end your day. This may include meditation, journaling, setting intentions, or engaging in self-care practices. These rituals create a sense of stability, grounding, and self-nurturing.

10.4.2 Mindful Eating: Bring mindfulness to your meals by savoring each bite, noticing the flavors and textures, and expressing gratitude for the nourishment. Eating mindfully enhances your connection with your body, promotes healthier choices, and deepens your appreciation for food.

10.4.3 Nature Connection: Spend time in nature regularly to foster a sense of connection and awe. Engage in mindful walks, observe the beauty of your surroundings, and connect with the natural rhythms. Nature has a way of grounding us and reminding us of our interconnectedness with all living beings.

By integrating the principles of guided meditation into your daily life, you transform your existence into a meditative journey of self-discovery, compassion, and inner peace. Embrace the wisdom and practices shared throughout this book and embark on a lifelong exploration of living a meditative life.

May your path be filled with serenity, joy, and profound inner transformation.

Conclusion

Congratulations on completing The Serene Path "The Art of Guided Meditation"! Throughout this book, we have delved into the profound practice of guided meditation, exploring its benefits, techniques, and applications in various aspects of life. We have journeyed through creating a sacred space, preparing for meditation, selecting the right techniques, and exploring different meditation themes. We have also examined how to overcome challenges, deepen our practice, and share the gift of guided meditation with others.

Remember that guided meditation is a personal journey, and each individual's experience will be unique. Embrace the flexibility and adaptability of this practice, allowing it to evolve and grow with you. The key is to approach your meditation practice with an open heart, a curious mind, and a commitment to self-care and personal growth.

As you embark on your guided meditation journey, I encourage you to cultivate a sense of patience and compassion towards yourself. Meditation is not about achieving perfection or attaining specific outcomes. It is a practice of presence and inner exploration, where the true beauty lies in the journey itself.

Appendix: Guided Meditation Scripts

To further support your practice, the appendix of this book provides a collection of guided meditation scripts. These scripts are designed to assist you in various areas of focus, including relaxation, mindfulness, self-discovery, and more. Feel free to adapt and customize these scripts to suit your personal preferences and the needs of your intended audience.

Resources for Further Exploration

To continue your exploration of guided meditation, consider exploring the following resources:

- Books: Dive deeper into the subject with books written by experienced meditation practitioners and teachers. Explore titles by renowned authors such as Jon Kabat-Zinn, Sharon Salzberg, Jack Kornfield, and Tara Brach.

- Meditation Apps: Utilize meditation apps that offer a wide range of guided meditations, mindfulness exercises, and helpful features. Some popular apps include Headspace, Calm, Insight Timer, and 10% Happier.

- Online Courses and Workshops: Seek out online courses and workshops on guided meditation and related topics. Many reputable meditation teachers and organizations offer virtual programs that allow you to deepen your knowledge and practice from the comfort of your own home.

- Local Meditation Communities: Connect with local meditation communities, centers, or groups in your area. Joining a community provides the opportunity to engage in group meditations, attend workshops, and connect with like-minded individuals who share your passion for meditation.

Acknowledgments

Writing this book would not have been possible without the support and contributions of numerous individuals. I would like to express my deepest gratitude to all the meditation teachers, authors, researchers, and practitioners who have dedicated their lives to the study and practice of guided meditation. Your wisdom and insights have greatly enriched this book.

I would also like to thank my editor and the entire publishing team for their guidance, expertise, and commitment to bringing this book to life. Your efforts are truly appreciated.

Finally, I extend my heartfelt appreciation to the readers of this book. It is my sincere hope that the knowledge and practices shared here will support you on your guided meditation journey, helping you find peace, clarity, and inner transformation. May your path be illuminated by the light of mindfulness and may your practice continue to blossom and flourish. May you experience the profound benefits of guided meditation in every aspect of your life.

Wishing you love, peace, and abundant joy on your continued journey of guided meditation.

With deepest gratitude,

Tamara Rucker-Wood

www.ingramcontent.com/pod-product-compliance
Lightning Source LLC
LaVergne TN
LVHW010622110826
845149LV00003B/1008

* 9 7 9 8 9 8 8 6 3 5 7 1 0 *